THE
KREPLACH NESS
MONSTER

To Felice (who said, "better you should write checks"), Di, and Nicole Je T'Aime

THE KREPLACH NESS MONSTER

AND OTHER PHRASES THAT DO NOT APPEAR IN *THE JOYS OF YIDDISH*, BUT SHOULD.*

*OR, WHAT BUBBE AND ZAYDE NEVER TAUGHT YOU

JAMES JOSEPH, LAWRENCE NASH AND THE WHOLE MISHPOCHEH

CONTEMPORARY
BOOKS, INC.
CHICAGO

This book is neither published, authored, sponsored, nor approved by the HBO television series "Not Necessarily the News" or by any persons connected therewith.

Acknowledgments

Arnold Chotiner, a real mensch, was with us from the start, giving support and encouragement. The following menschen and womenschen have helped with the whole megilla and kvellify for some kovid: Rick and Diane Lauber, Michael Yamin, D. A. Hudak, Jeremy, Benjamin, Sylvia, Norene, V. S. Sandifer, Tabitha, Ziggie, Abe Vinikoor, Terry Fincham, Valerie Zeller, Dan Cherkin, Wendie Bramwell, Jeff and Deni Bauman, Dan and Lassie Webster, John Silverman, Julie Silverman, Amy Berdann, Felice Joseph, William N. Gordon, Leonard and Bernice Gordon, Sandy and Doris Slavin, Jeffry Slavin, Roni and Peter Pekins, Susan Freed Gordon, Jimmy Gordon, Jerry and Mabel Gordon, Steve and Judy Greenberg, Carl and Sondra Goldenberg, Rose Saperstein, Mark Greenfield, Barry Sarles, Neil Sarles, and Lisa Wickersham. A shainen dank. If there's any kvetching to do about this book, take it up with Morris the Katz.

afikoments

(*ahf ee* **KAH** *ments*) *n*. Adult arguing that occurs as children search for the hidden Passover matzo.

agnoshtik

(*ag* **NOSH** *tik*) *n*. One who doubts that chicken soup can cure a cold.

ambifresstic

(*am bee* **FRES** *tik*) *adj* Having the ability to eat hors d'oeuvres with both hands while maintaining a conversation.

anchors oyvey

(ANG *kors oy* VAY) *n.* Saying attributed to the rabbi on the *Titanic*. Today it means, "ever since the *Titanic* went down, I don't go out on boats (but you go and have fun)." (*See **baruch ahoy**.*)

ashcanape

(*ash can a* **PAY**) *n*. An unidentifiable pastry found at a reception that you don't eat until you've seen another person eat one like it without **bissecting** it (*see* **bissect**).

ashkeshnozzola

(*osh ka shna* **ZO** *lah*) *n*. A nose the shape of Florida and the size of a medium potato.

bagela

(**BAY** *g'l ah*) *n*. A gay Jewish baker.

bageloxitis

(*bay g'l ok* **STI** *tis*) *n*. An affliction caused by the inability to find a delicatessen within a twenty-mile radius; symptoms include a sudden urge to call one's mother, rapid eye twitching brought on by constant, futile searching for a subway, and a hoarseness from saying "you know, *smoked salmon*," one too many times.

WELCOME TO PODUNKVILLE POR 363

NEXT BAGEL 28 MILES

barmittance

(*bar* **MIT** *entz*) *n*. Inviting people to your son's bar mitzvah who invited you to their sons bar mitzvah.

barmitzushi

(*bar mit* **ZUSH** *ee*) *n*. Traditional post-yontif fare consisting of herring, salmon, and tuna in bizarre-shaped molds (so why are you paying so much to eat in a fancy foreign restaurant? Our fish isn't good enough for you?).

baruch ahoy

(*bar* **UKH** *ah* **HOY**) *n*. Rabbi to the starboard (*see* **anchors oyvey**).

basebagel

(*bays* **BAY** *g'l*) *n*. A stick game played in college with a four-day-old bagel.

bialy ache

(*bee* **AHL** *ee ayk*) *n*. The result of lunch at your mother's and dinner at your mother-in law's.

B

bialy button

(*bee* **AHL** *ee* **BUH** *ton*) *n*. The large crater-like depression in a bialy.

bissect

(*bis* **EHKT**) *vb* To take only one bite from an hors d'oeuvre or pastry and nonchalantly abandon it on the buffet table (**bissected** food is a major component of a **bisscombobulated** table and is most noticeable when you arrive late and hungry).

bisshlepper

(*bis* **SHLEP** *pur*) *n*. One whose offers of help are always preceded by "I don't mind even though my back . . ." (and who always ends up carrying the empty boxes, the lampshades, the pillows, and the dried flowers).

B

blintzkrieg

(BLINTS *kreeg*) *n.* A late-night assault on the refrigerator in search of leftovers even though "I won't be able to eat for a week!"; particularly common 4–6 hours after special occasion gluttony.

bopkisses

(*bop* **KIS** *iz*) *n*. The actions of two strangers intimately greeting each other by simultaneously pecking the air near each other's cheeks.

bris and tell

(*briss and tehl*) *n*. A detailed description given by parents of their child's circumcision, generally spoken quite loudly in front of the grown child and those people he would least like to hear the story.

bronxodus

(BRONKS *oh dis*) *n*. Whole neighborhoods moving uptown or to the suburbs to make room for the next boatload.

brooklint

(BROOK *lint*) *n*. The dust and dirt that collects in one's inner-city apartment before one moves to the air-conditioned clean comfort of the suburbs.

bubbegum

(*bub* **EH** *gum*) *n*. Candy one's mother gives to her grandchildren that she never gave to her own children.

bubbetition

(*bub eh* **TIH** *shun*) *n*. The art of restructuring a basic concept in an immeasurable number of ways during the course of one encounter, as in, "Don't you *like* girls? Don't you *want* a family? So how much are you making now . . . *that's* not enough to feed *two* people? Have you seen Frankie's new baby yet? Oh, wasn't *that* a beautiful wedding? Have you met Mildred's granddaughter yet? W*hat* a lovely girl."

B

B

bubbevision

(*bub eh* **VI** *shun*) *n.*
The ability to imagine a
three-year-old as a
world famous
neurosurgeon.

chaseride

(*khaz* **EH** *ride*) *vb* To share a car with one who uses the back seat for storage, the front seat as an ash tray and the road as a garbage can.

chatchkart

(**CHACH** *kart*) *n.* The tray on wheels in an elderly person's apartment that holds metal pill boxes and compacts, ceramic statues (some with clocks; some with music boxes that play "Sunrise, Sunset") and other things no one has looked at since they were bought.

chazolerie

(*khaz* **OH** *ler ee*) *n.* The unit of energy needed to burn off a full meal from one's mother's table (roughly equivalent to what a nuclear power plant generates in half a day).

chianxiety

(*khi ankst I eh tee*) *n.* The state of mind of a young college student reviewing his or her life plans to figure out the easiest and most enjoyable way to become a doctor, lawyer, or a chief executive officer.

ch'mute

(*kh'MEWT*) *n.* The inability to pronounce the "kh" sound (one who can use it is a *ch'municator*).

chutzpapa

(**KHUTS** *pah pah*) *n.* A father who wakes his wife at 4 A.M. so she can change the baby's diaper.

circumcisual

(**sir com SIZ u ahl**) *adj* Anything done in a cutting manner.

crosshmeered

(**kros SHMEAR'D**) *vb* To receive at least six identical pen and pencil sets for your bar mitzvah.

deja nu

(**DAY** *jah new*) *n.* Having the feeling you've seen the same exasperated look on your mother's face but not knowing exactly when.

democratz

(***dem oh* KRATS**) *n.* One who aligns himself/herself politically with the party he/she enjoys complaining the most about ("If only FDR were alive").

discahkentude

(***dis* KOK *en tewd***) *n.* Looking like one isn't involved while one's dog goes to the bathroom on a neighbor's lawn.

diskvellified

(**dis** **KVE** *lih fide*) *vb* To drop out of law school, med school or business school, as seen through the eyes of parents, grandparents, and Uncle Sid (In extreme cases, simply choosing to major in art history when Irv's son David is majoring in biology is sufficient grounds for diskvellification.).

disoriyenta

(**dis** *oar ee* **YEN** *tah*) *n.* When Aunt Sadie gets lost in a department store and strikes up conversation with everyone she passes.

D

dr. schlock

(DOK *tor shlok*) *n*. A pediatrician whose advice is rejected by his own mother.

drecklect

(DREK *lekt*) *vb* To use dirty words in Yiddish in front of people who have no idea what they mean.

elalienation

(*el ahl ee en* **AY** *shun*) *n*. An aversion to flying on El Al airlines.

emystical

(*eh* **MIS** *tik al*) *adj* Answering a question with a question in order to evade the issue and confound the questioner.

essentales

(*ess* **EN** *taylz*) *n*. Myths repeated at mealtime, originating from the existence of uneaten food or refused second helpings. EX. 1: The myth of the invisible trans-continental transfer of already-eaten food (*e.g.* food consumed at American dinner tables prevents starvation in the third world). EX. 2: The myth of the wonder foods—foods which magically alter the appearance of their consumer, such as causing eyes to sparkle, hair to grow on ten-year-old chests and, occasionally, trees to grow in bellies.

esstute

(**es TEWT**) *adj* Knowing which hors d'oeuvres taste best at a reception even though they're made from livers, gizzards, raw fish, mystery meat, and vegetables only heard of in the old country.

farkvetched

(**far K'VECH'D**) *vb*. To exaggerate a minor complaint to the point where it is portrayed as a capital crime, such as, "If you don't stop parking in front of my house, I'm calling the FBI."

feelawful

(*feel* AW *ful*) *n.* Indigestion from eating Israeli street food.

fleishadick

(FLAYSH *ah dik*) *n.* A Jewish flasher.

F

freuday

(**FROY** *day*) *n*. The day of the week one regularly schedules for psychoanalysis.

gefilt-ello

(*geh* **FILT** *el oh*) *n*. The gelatinous substance found in gefilte fish jars. (*See* **surgelfiltery**.)

geltgate

(**GELT** *gayt*) *n*. The barrier that prevents one from spending all one's money "in one place" or "until you're old enough" or "so when you go to college, you'll have a little something."

gematrimonia

(*geh mah tree* **MOAN** *ee ah*) *n*. The mystical prediction of how long a marriage will last made by counting the carats in an engagement ring.

gevalteration

(*geh volt er* **AY shun**) *n.* What happens to one's wool sweater when it goes through the wrong cycle at the dry cleaners. **Gevaltered** clothes often make good baby gifts.

gladkosher

(*glad* **KOH** *shur*) *n.* Delight in finding a delicatessen in Norfolk, Nebraska. Gladkosher is the only cure known for ***bageloxitis***.

gonifinicky

(*gaw nih* **FIH** *nih kee*) *n.* A thief who cares to steal the very best.

gonifishing

(*gaw ni* **FI** *shing*) *n.* What happens to the business when one of the partners goes on vacation.

goyfer

(**GOY** *fur*) *n.* A gentile messenger.

goymet food

(*goy* **MAY** *fewd*) *n.* Cheez Whiz, bologna and mayo on white bread with milk; anything at a fish fry.

guiltgelt

(**GILT** *gelt*) *n.* The money grandparents slip under the table after parents refuse a tear-jerking request (generally occurs only the first time grandparents have heard the tear-jerking request).

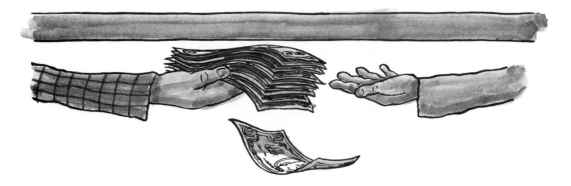

haltzflicknik

(*halts* **FLIK** *nik*) *n*. Someone who has seen every Woody Allen film.

hannukitch

(*khan u* **KICH**) *n*. Hannukah decorations colored green and red to blend with Christmas ornaments.

hebort

(**HEE** *bort*) *vb* To forget all the Hebrew one ever learned, immediately after one's bar mitzvah.

hebrute

(*hee* **BREWT**) *n*. Israeli aftershave.

hindstein

(**HIND** *stine*) *n.* A Semitic smartass.

horantics

(*hor* **AN** *tiks*) *n.* The chain collision caused by one klutz while dancing the *Hora*, and the subsequent attempts to untangle from this disaster.

hunkela

(**HUNK** *eh lah*) *n.* The standard unit of measure for putting cream cheese on a bagel; beyond *triple-hunkela* and you're putting bagel on cream cheese.

impasta

(*im* **PAS** *tah*) *n*. Someone who eats leavened foods during Passover while maintaining he/she is observant.

interior drekoration

(*in* **TIR** *ee ur drek ur* **AY** *shun*) *n*. The placement of spillproof, translucent, heavy vinyl over living room furnishings so as to render those furnishings completely unidentifiable (but what are you complaining about? you're not allowed in the living room anyway).

isroyalty

(*iz* **ROY** *al tee*) *n.* Major financial contributors to the UJA, the JUF, or the IEF.

jewbilation

(*joo bil* **AY** *shun*) *n.* Pride in finding out that one's favorite celebrity is Jewish.

jewdo

(**JU** *doh*) *n.* A traditional form of self defense based on talking one's way out of a tight spot.

jubiliddish

(*jew bih* **LID** *ish*) *n*. The language a mother uses to describe her son, the doctor.

kibbizness

(*kih* **BIZ** *nis*) *n*. Gratuitious advice, usually unasked for, on how to run a business.

kibbutsick

(*kee* **BUTS** *ik*) *n*. Illness brought on by an inability to handle kibbutz life; primary symptom being the inability to rise at 4 A.M. to pick bananas.

kinderschlep

(**kin der SHLEP**) *vb* To be called on to carpool more children than one has fingers, in a car that was made in Japan.

knadlrock

(*kin* AYD *ul rok*) *n.* A dumpling that has been reheated more than four times.

koptortions

(*kop* **TOR** *shunz*) *n*. The positions one has to hold one's head so that one's yarmulkah won't fall into one's dinner. An expert of this technique is called a *koptortionist*.

kreplach ness monster

(*krep* LAKH *nes Mon stir*) *n*. Any doting relative who won't let you leave the table until you have eaten twelve dumplings.

kvell-o-gram

(K'VEL *oh gram***)** *n.* A notice or announcement of a special event from a parent to anyone who will receive it. It can read like this: My Irving just graduated Harvard Law School. Is your Morris out of jail yet? Love Sadie.

kvetch 22

(*k'vech* **22)** *n.* When your mother asks you incessantly to fix up your cousin Mildred (the one with the wonderful personality) with your friend Bob (the one with the wicked right hook).

kvetchmarks

(K'VECH *marx***)** *n.* The crow's-feet and wrinkled foreheads that come from saying "you spent how much?!" too often.

leaftmensh

(*leeft mench*) *n*. Job-title of the person who puts the bay leaf in jars of herring.

lichtouts

(**LIKT** *owts*) *n*. Running out of Hannukah candles.

mamatzah balls

(*mah* **MAHT** *suh balz*) *n*. Matzo balls that are as good as mother used to make.

matza-matta?

(**MAHT** *suh* **MOT** *ah*) *slang* What Irving Schwartz said to Luigi Pasaluqua when something went wrong (still a greeting used in Italian-Jewish neighborhoods).

matzamold

(**MAHT** *suh mold*) *n.* Finding the afikomin four months too late.

matza-shmata

(**MAHT** *suh* **SHMAH** *tuh*) *adj* Having so much starch in one's clothing that one feels like one's underwear might break into little pieces.

matzilation

(*maht zil AY shun*) *n.* Smashing a piece of matzo to bits while trying to butter it.

mazuma's revenge

(*mah ZEW mahz REE venj*) *n.* Indigestion brought on by another bad day in the stock market or eating lunch with a banker.

meinstein

(**MINE** *stine*) *slang* "My son, the genius."

menshkin

(**MENCH** *kin*) *n.* A mensh-in-training; *e.g.* one who helps mom after dinner by putting the fine crystal in the dishwasher and scouring the fine china with Ajax cleanser.

meshugaga

(*mesh* **UH** *gah gah*) *n*. The way grandparents have when brought into contact with new grandchildren.

meshujogger

(*mesh* **UH** *jah gur*) *n*. A person who puts make-up on to jog.

metsiamaniac

(*mets ee ah* MAYN *ee ak*) *n.* [1]. A person who is unable to pass up anything on sale, easily identified by the possession of a twenty-five year supply of shampoo. 2. A person unable to drive past a garage sale without browsing and buying at least a twenty-five cent item as their contribution to the perpetuation of garage sales everywhere.

miambience

(*my* AM *bee ants*) *n.* The atmosphere, climate, and environment older people feel comfortable retiring to after long years in northern cities.

mezupeek

(*mez* **EW** *peek*) *n*. The uncontrollable urge to see what's inside a mezuzah.

minyastics

(*min* YAS *tiks*) *n.* Going to incredible lengths and troubles to find a tenth person to complete a minyan. (Also, *see* **ninyan** *and* **tzenhere**.)

mishpochamarks

(*mish* POKH *ah marx*) *n.* The assorted lipstick and make-up stains found on one's face and collars after kissing all one's aunts and cousins at a reception.

moganchuck

(MOH *gan chuk*) *n.* Illness from drinking cheap wine.

morris the katz

(MOR *is thuh cats*) *n*. A feline. Easily identified by two sets of bowls and cigar; can generally be found in warm, dry climates during the winter months.

nastipunim

(*na* **STI** *pun im*) *n.* A face only a mother could love.

nebash

(**NEB** *ash*) *n.* A party given for nerds.

ninyan

(**NIN** *yun*) *n.* The nine people of a minyan waiting for the tenth person to show up. (*See also* **minyastics** *and* **tzenhere**.)

nudeneck

(**NEWD** *nek*) *n.* A person with an open collar at a formal party. (Often a large collar mistaken for a pair of wings.)

outbech

(*owt* **BEKH**) *n*. Where the person in a bakery that's not present when they call his/her number is hiding.

oydable

(**OY** *da bil*) *adj* Complaining done with just enough noise to get everyone's attention: "Don't worry about me, I'll just walk to the airport."

oy gestalt!

(*oy ges* **TALT**) *n*. The reaction of a mother when she learns her child is in group therapy to determine whether or not he or she is gay.

o

paranoshoid

(*par ah* **NOSH** *oyd*) *n.* One who will never take seconds during dinner but always volunteers to clear the table *alone* and spends three hours choosing the right containers for the mysteriously dwindled leftovers.

passodor

(*pas* **OH** *dor*) *n.* Mysterious scent permeating suburban condominium hallways each spring.

petrishugana

(*peh tree* **SHUH** *gah nah*) *n.* Driving ten miles across town to save a penny on the price of gasoline.

phdumkopf

(*fi* **DOOM** *kopff*) *n.* A person with a doctorate on the wall and a hackney's license in the wallet.

photsuris

(*fo* **TSUR** *is*) *n.* Finding out that the best photos from one's wedding, bar mitzvah or family reunion are those of people one had hoped would not even show up.

pish-ups

(*pish ups*) *vb* To get a daily workout from picking up after one's kids.

procresstinate

(*pro* **KRES** *tin ayt*) *vb* To decide perpetually to start a diet tomorrow.

punimpincher

(*pun im* **PIN** *chur*) *n.* A person who cannot greet a person without pinching their cheeks; punimpinching, although painful, rarely leaves visible scars.

pupiclean

(*pup* IH *kleen*) *n*. An obsession with removing lint from one's belly button. One who enjoys this process is a ***pupicleadanist***.

rechupparate

(*ree* KHUP *er ayt*) *n*. Two divorcees getting married, also known as a triumph of hope over experience.

reinschpiel

(REE *in shpeel*) *vb* To drag out the same lines on your children that your parents used on you because you can't think of anything original to say. For example, "because I said so and I'm your mother," "I'm not asking, I'm telling."

repupicans

(*re* **POOP** *ee kanz*) *n*. People who vote with their stomach, such as, "Is this dinner tax deductible?" and, "Can I afford five cases of Dom Perignon or only four?"

reshtetlement

(*ree* **SHTET** *el ment*) *n*. Moving from Brooklyn to Miami and finding all your old neighbors live in the same condo as you.

resumacher

(*rez u* **MAKH** *ur*) *n*. Someone who has impressive credentials on paper but can't deliver results in real life.

riddadakinder

(**rid ah dah KIN dur**) *n*. The annual practice of sending the kids to Camp Ramah or Blue Star.

rosh hashanana

(*rosh hah* **SHAH** *nah nah*) *n.* A rock 'n' roll band from Brooklyn.

sankvetch

(*sank'vech*) *n.* Any complainer before his or her first cup of coffee.

santashmanta

(**San** *tah* **SHMAN** *tah*) *n.* The explanation Jewish children get for why they celebrate Hannukah while the rest of humanity celebrates Christmas.

schlerm

(*shlurm*) *n.* The wrinkled end of a Hebrew National salami.

schmucker

(**SHMUH** *kur*) *n.* Any name from the old country, before it was changed, that no one can remember (or that their grandfather refuses to tell them). "With a name like that, it had to be bad."

schmuckluck

(*shmuh* **KLUK**) *n*. Finding out
one's wife became pregnant
after one had a vasectomy.

schnozle-tov

(**SHNOZ** *el tof*) *n.* What one says to someone who just had a good nose-job.

sederapid

(*say dur* **AP** *id*) *n.* The satiating result of inviting a master hagaddah-editor to Passover dinner.

shalope

(**SHAH** *lope*) *vb* Running away to get married to keep the two families from going to war over the wedding arangements.

sheleprities

(*shel* **EP** *ri teez*) *n.* People who become famous for things a normal person would not want to be known for, such as criminals, sex symbols, colossal failures, and advertising executives.

shiksabob

(SHIK *suh bob*) *n*. A special meal that Muffy McGreggor prepares for Morris Greenblatt.

ל

shlock therapy

(*shlok* **THER** *uh pee*) *n*. Forcing one's family to shop in discount chain department stores so they will learn the value of money.

shmatyester

(*shmat ee* **ESS** *tur*) *n*. Cheap material or synthetic cloth used in inexpensive clothing that no self-respecting person wears.

shmegociations

(*shmah goh shee* **AY** *shuns*) *n*. Attempts to make your mother-in-law like you.

shofarsogut

(*sho* **FAR** *sew gewt*) *n*. The relief you feel when after many attempts the shofar is finally blown at the end of Yom Kippur.

shtik-up

(**SHTIK** *up*) *vb* To steal someone else's puns.

shvigure

(**SHVI** *gur*) *n*. The amount of money one's mother-in-law says one should make to support her child properly. Usually quite a bit more than one can hope to make.

shylox

(**SHY** *loks*) *n*. A blunderous miscalculation of the quantity of smoked salmon needed for the Sunday brunch.

sighnye

(**SY** *ny*) *n*. A mother's daily sigh, quite useful in guilt-perpetuation maneuvers.

smelling schmaltz

(**SMEL** *ing* **SHMALTS**) *n*. Chicken noodle soup strategically positioned within olfactory range of a cold-stricken individual; guaranteed to revive the stuffiest of noses.

strudelegate

(*strew* **DEL** *eh gayt*) *vb* To choose a dessert and a person to bake it for a pot luck dinner.

sureshlock homes

(**SHUR** *shlok homz*) *n*. Neighborhoods a decent person would never live in.

surgefiltery

(*sur geh* **FIL** *ter ee*) *vb* To remove delicately the goo attached to gefilte fish without touching the stuff. (*See* ***gefilt-ello***.)

synago-go

(*sin* AH *goh goh*) *n.* A dance given by the youth group.

synaroma

(*sin ah* ROH *mah*) *n.* The delicious but disconcerting smell of food wafting through *shul* at the end of a long service (particularly noticeable during the Yom Kippur fast).

tallastics

(*tahl* AS *tiks*) *n.* The jumping jack type movements it takes to get one's prayer shawl on properly.

technoschmendrick

(*tek no* **SHMEN** *drik*) *n.* A person who buys a $10,000 computer to balance his or her checkbook or to store recipes.

thegoysofyiddish

(*thuh goyz ov* **YID** *ish*) *n.* When gentiles use or misuse Jewish words and expressions to impress or depress their Jewish friends. As in "Congratulations Bennie, I hear you married a *shiksa*; your mother must be so happy."

theprincessprinciple

(*thuh prin se* **SPRIN** *sih pull*) *n.* Daddy will buy it for me.

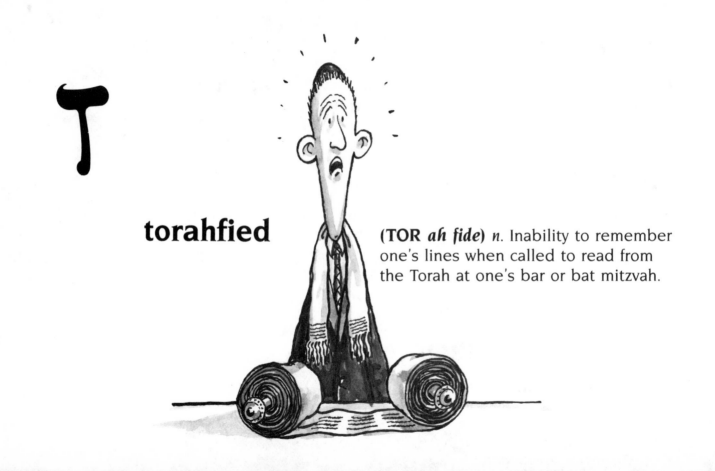

torahfied

(TOR *ah fide***)** *n.* Inability to remember one's lines when called to read from the Torah at one's bar or bat mitzvah.

traumavic

(*traw* **MAY** *vik*) *n*. Disgruntlement from knowing more about a subject than one's mother, but losing the argument anyway because, "I'm your mother."

trayfart

(**TRAY** *fart*) *n*. Gas pains from eating non-kosher food. Usually accompanies a *trayffic accident*.

trayffic accident

(**TRAY** *fik* **AK** *sih dent*) *n*. An appetizer one finds out has pork in it after one has eaten it. Often causes *trayfarts*.

tzenzhere

(*tsen* **HERE**) *n*. The tenth person who finally shows up for a minyan. (See *minyastics* and *ninyan*.)

tzorinstant

(*tsour* IN *stants*) *n.* The moment one realizes he's in big trouble. For example, when the IRS calls about the business trip to Mazatlan or when one calls his wife "Mimi," and her name is "Ruth."

weiss guy

(*wyzz guy*) *n.* Anybody who would eat good pastrami, corned beef, salami, or roast beef on Wonder Bread with mayonnaise and a sweet pickle.

yentility

(*yen* **TIL** *ih tee*) *n*. A deceptively sweet manner used to extract information. Key phrases include, "trust me," "your secret is safe with me" and, "if you can't tell me, who can you tell?"

yidentify

(*yi* **DENT** *ih fy*) *vb* To be able to determine ethnic origins of celebrities even though their names might be St. John, Curtis, Davis, or Taylor.

the yontif gonif

(*thuh* YON *tiff* GON *if*) *n*. The grinch who stole Hannukah.

zaftickle

(*zaf* TIK *el*) *v*. To find the one fleshy spot on every person's body which, no matter how gruff or grouchy they might be, when touched, collapses them into hysterical laughter. The point is referred to as the Z-*Schpot*.

zaydelation

z

(*zayd el* **AY** *shun*) *n*. The feeling a grandfather has when he hears that his grandchild's first words are "Harvard Medical School."

The Original Kreplach Ness Monster Card

So Nu,

How could you schlemiels do this book without my favorite word? Here, you'll appreciate my shtik; it's better than some of the chazerei you used in this book (and use it in good health):

_____

_____

_____

_____

_____

Listen, if you hindsteins are such mavens, why hok me a chainek? Lechaim,

_____

_____

_____

_____

Name

Address

Send reply to: Jim Joseph
c/o Contemporary Books, Inc.
180 N. Michigan Ave.
Chicago, IL 60601